Fact Finders®

DISCOVER THE NIGHT SKY

EXPLORING ECLIPSES

BY JILL SHERMAN

Consultant:
Ilia Iankov Roussev, PhD

CAPSTONE PRESS
a capstone imprint

Fact Finders Books are published by Capstone Press,
1710 Roe Crest Drive, North Mankato, Minnesota 56003
www.mycapstone.com

Copyright © 2018 by Capstone Press, a Capstone imprint. All rights reserved. No part of this
publication may be reproduced in whole or in part, or stored in a retrieval system, or transmitted
in any form or by any means, electronic, mechanical, photocopying, recording, or otherwise,
without written permission of the publisher.

Library of Congress Cataloging-in-Publication Data
Library of Congress Cataloging-in-Publication data is available on the Library of Congress website.

978-1-5157-8736-5 (library binding)
978-1-5157-8740-2 (paperback)
978-1-5157-8752-5 (eBook PDF)

Editorial Credits
Adrian Vigliano, editor; Veronica Scott, designer;
Wanda Winch, media researcher; Gene Bentdahl, production specialist

Photo Credits
Alamy Stock Photo: Hemis, 23 (bottom), Ivy Close Images, 7 (top), Photo Researchers, Inc., 21 (b);
Dreamstime: Astrobobo, 18–19, Igorfp, 28; iStockphoto: adventtr, 8–9; Newscom: Reuters/David Gray,
26–27; Science Source: Claus Lunau, 25; Shutterstock: BlueRingMedia, 11, Chiradech Chotchaung, 29,
Dr. Ajay Kumar Singh, 10, Georgios Kollidas, 7 (b), Igor Zh., cover, NikoNomad, 22–23 (background),
Pavel Vakhrushev, starfield background, Pi-Lens, 5, Tom Tietz, 13 (bottom right), Viliam.M, 16–17
(background); Thinkstock: iStockphoto/demarfa, 21 (t), iStockphoto/NdRphotographer, 17 (b),
iStockphoto/SMJoness, 12–13 (background), iStockphoto/solarseven, 15

Printed in China.
010293F17

TABLE OF CONTENTS

CHAPTER 1

WHAT IS AN ECLIPSE?

The night sky is full of stars. You can see the moon and sometimes other planets too. They may look still, but these objects are in constant motion. As our Earth moves through space, new objects come into view. Others are blocked.

When one object in space moves into the shadow of another, that's an **eclipse**. The second object is no longer totally visible. It is still there. It is just hiding in shadow.

The most common eclipses that we see are of the sun and moon. Earth **orbits** the sun, and the moon orbits Earth. When their orbits align, they cast shadows. The shadows create an eclipse. It is a stunning event to see.

eclipse—when one object in space blocks light and keeps it from shining on another object in space
orbit—path an object follows as it goes around the sun or a planet

FIRST RECORDS

Ancient people watched the sun, moon, and stars. They used the movements to make calendars. When these objects seemed to disappear, it was an important event. The earliest records of eclipses were made in China. They date back more than 4,000 years. Chinese scientists studied the patterns. This helped them predict future eclipses.

Still, the cause of an eclipse was a mystery. They became part of **mythology**. Norse tribes believed a giant wolf ate the sun during an eclipse. Hindus described serpents that suck away the sun's light.

Eclipses were also considered a bad omen. Ancient Greeks believed it meant a disaster was coming. It was also a bad sign for rulers. In Babylon, fake kings were put on the throne during eclipses. This was meant to protect the real rulers from harm.

mythology—old or ancient stories told again and again that help connect people with their past

Did You Know?

In AD 1133 there was an eclipse in Britain. King Henry I died shortly after. The eclipse lasted 4 minutes and 38 seconds. It's known as King Henry's Eclipse. The king's death seemed like a sure sign that eclipses meant danger.

King Henry I

CHAPTER 2

WHEN DOES AN ECLIPSE OCCUR?

Eclipses are not common events. The Earth and moon cast shadows into space as they make their orbit. On Earth we can't usually see the shadows. We can only see the shadows when objects such as the sun, Earth, and moon cross paths in a straight line.

Sometimes the moon passes directly between Earth and sun. The moon blocks the light from the sun. It casts a shadow on Earth. For people standing in the shadow, the sun has been blocked out. The area passes into darkness. This event is called a **solar eclipse**. The sun was blocked out from view.

Other times, Earth will pass directly between the sun and moon. Earth blocks sunlight from reaching the moon. This blocks the moon. This event is a **lunar eclipse**.

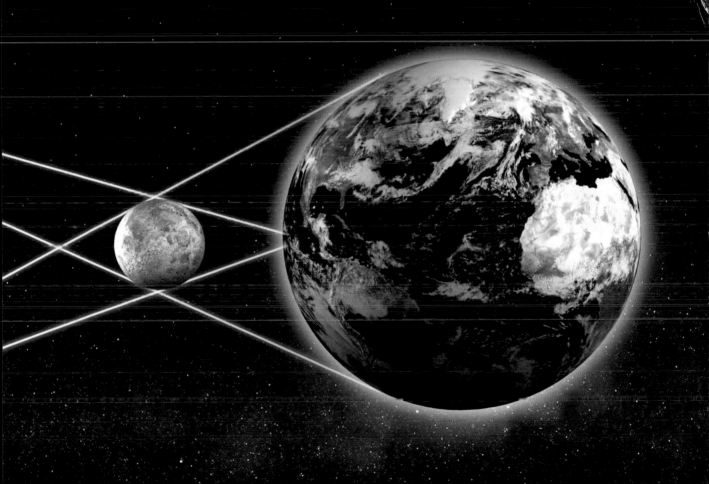

solar eclipse—astronomical event in which the moon passes between the sun and Earth
lunar eclipse—astronomical event in which Earth's shadow passes over the moon

LUNAR ECLIPSES

A lunar eclipse happens only during the night of a full moon. On these nights the entire face of the moon is lit. Then Earth passes between the sun and the moon. Earth eclipses the moon. Its shadow covers the moon.

There are two types of lunar eclipses — total and partial. In a partial eclipse, the sun, Earth, and moon are almost, but not perfectly, in line. Only part of the moon enters Earth's shadow. A dark shadow passes over the moon's surface.

Partial Eclipse

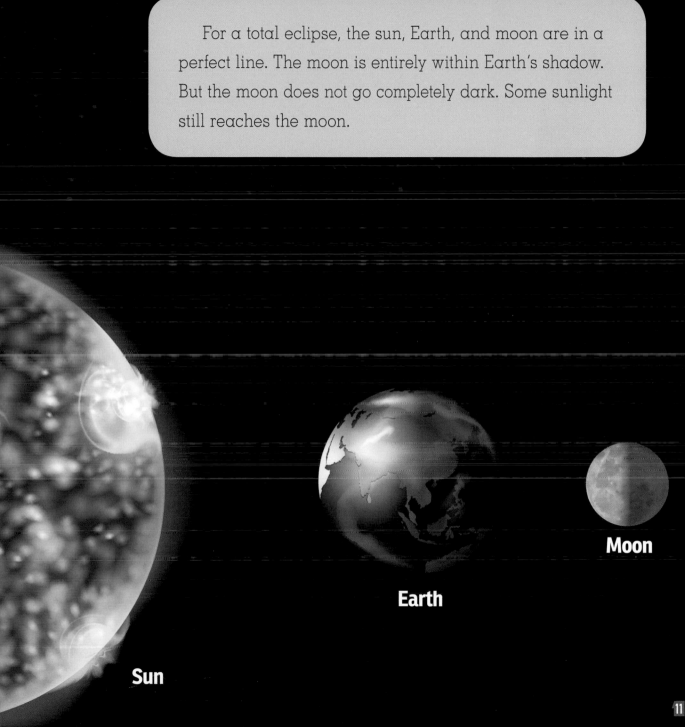

For a total eclipse, the sun, Earth, and moon are in a perfect line. The moon is entirely within Earth's shadow. But the moon does not go completely dark. Some sunlight still reaches the moon.

Moon

Earth

Sun

Sunlight is made up of different kinds of light. It contains all the colors of the rainbow. Light from the sun passes through Earth's atmosphere. It acts like a lens. The air bends the light. It separates into different colors. Red light bends. Some of it reaches the moon. So the moon takes on a red color during an eclipse.

The exact color of the moon during an eclipse can change a little. Temperature, humidity, or a recent volcanic eruption can change how the light bends. This is the same reason that some sunsets vary in shades of red, orange, and gold. In an eclipse, the moon may show shades of red, orange, gold, or pink.

Usually, a lunar eclipse lasts for a few hours. There are about two partial eclipses every year. Total lunar eclipses occur about once every 18 months. They are visible wherever it's nighttime on Earth.

Did You Know?

A lunar eclipse is often called a "blood moon." In ancient times a blood moon was often seen as a bad omen. It was thought to signal the end times.

SOLAR ECLIPSES

When the moon comes between Earth and the sun, it blocks out the sun's light. The moon eclipses the sun. A shadow is cast on Earth. A solar eclipse occurs. Solar eclipses occur about every 18 months. They last only a few minutes. Solar eclipses are visible only in a narrow path on Earth's surface. The path is less than 186 miles (300 kilometers) wide. There are three types of solar eclipses. They are total, partial, and annular eclipses.

A total eclipse can only be seen from a small area on Earth. The people in that spot see the moon's shadow. The shadow hits the Earth, blocking out sunlight. The sun is completely covered. The sky gets dark. Only a thin halo of light peeks out from behind the moon. The sun, moon, and Earth must be exactly in line for a total eclipse to occur.

A partial eclipse happens when the sun, moon, and Earth are almost lined up. The moon covers part of the sun. The sun looks like a crescent. It's like someone took a bite out of it.

During an annular eclipse, the moon passes directly in front of the sun. But it does not cover the sun completely. Sometimes the moon's orbit takes it closer to Earth than others. Sometimes it is farther away. When the moon is closer, it looks larger. It can cover the entire sun. When the moon is farther away, it looks smaller. It does not block the whole sun. A dark circle covers the center of the sun. A bright ring glows around the dark center.

Partial Solar Eclipse

PARTS OF THE ECLIPSE

During a solar eclipse, the moon casts two shadows on Earth. The first shadow is the umbra. It gets smaller as it reaches Earth. The umbra is the dark center of the moon's shadow. Sunlight is completely blocked.

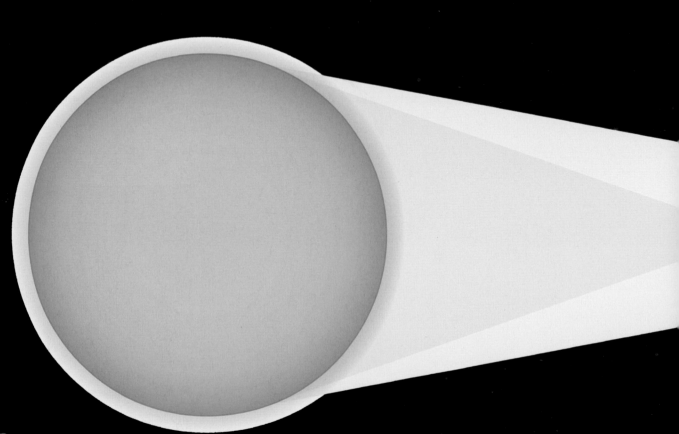

The second shadow is the penumbra. This shadow gets larger as it reaches Earth. It surrounds the umbra. Sunlight is partly blocked. It casts a lighter shadow.

Only a small area of Earth falls in the umbra of an eclipse. The area is just 186 miles (300 km) wide. The shadow sweeps across Earth's surface. It travels west to east. People in the shade of the umbra will see a total eclipse. People in the penumbra will see a partial eclipse.

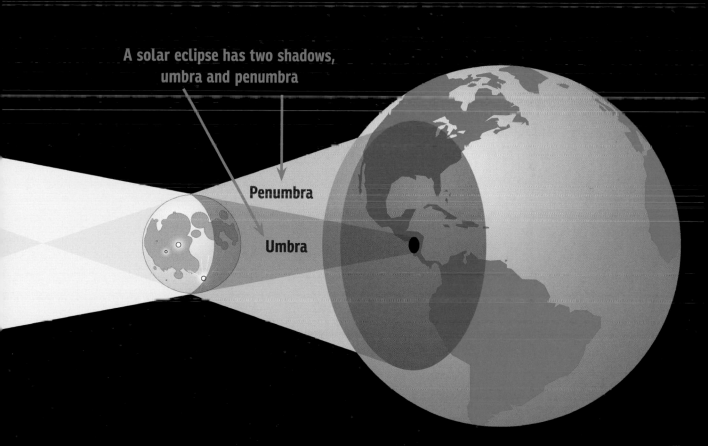

A solar eclipse has two shadows, umbra and penumbra

Penumbra

Umbra

OTHER ECLIPSES

Not all eclipses are of the sun, moon, and Earth. Two planets come between Earth and the sun. They are Mercury and Venus. The planets form an eclipse called a transit. They travel across the face of the sun. From Earth the planets look like small black dots. Transits are very rare. Over a span of 100 years, there are only about 13 transits of Mercury. During that time Venus transits just twice.

Astronomers also observe eclipses on other planets. Jupiter and its moons have lunar and solar eclipses. When a moon or planet blocks light from a distant star that is also an eclipse. Any kind of eclipse can help scientists better understand space.

astronomer—scientist who studies stars, planets, and other objects in space

Venus Transit

The Speed of Light

In 1675 Olaus Roemer was studying eclipses on Jupiter. He measured how long the eclipses lasted. A moon would disappear behind Jupiter. But it did not always take the same time to reappear. Roemer found that the time depended on how close Earth was to Jupiter. The time difference showed that light traveled with speed. He calculated the speed of light. It moves very fast. Light travels at 186,000 miles (299,792 km) per second.

CHAPTER 3

ECLIPSE SCIENCE

Eclipses give scientists a unique look at the night sky. Every eclipse lets them learn more. Space agencies around the world study eclipses. In the United States that agency is NASA.

In 2011 NASA sent an **orbiter** to study an eclipse. It measured the change in the moon's temperature. This helped scientists figure out what the moon's surface is made of. They also learned about the terrain. Smooth surfaces cool more quickly. Rough surfaces take longer to cool.

During a solar eclipse, NASA studies the sun's **corona**. This is the sun's outer atmosphere. It is very faint. It is only visible during an eclipse. Scientists hope to learn how the corona affects Earth.

Coronagraph

Scientists are very interested in the corona. But waiting for a solar eclipse takes a long time. That is why scientists created the coronagraph. It is a special type of telescope. It mimics a solar eclipse. Now scientists can view the corona any time. The device also has other uses. Today, they are used to discover far away **exoplanets**.

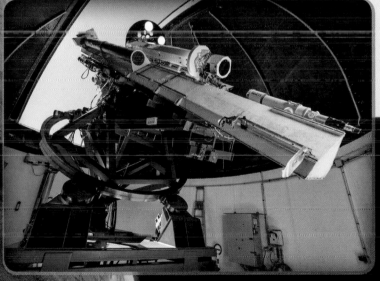

orbiter—spacecraft that orbits a planet or other space objects

corona—when one object in space blocks light and keeps it from shining on another object in space

exoplanet—planet that orbits a star outside the solar system

DISCOVERIES FROM ECLIPSES

Solar eclipses have led to some great discoveries. During an 1868 eclipse, scientists saw a yellow line in the sun's spectrum. It was not made by any known **element**. They named the new element after the Greek God of the sun, Helios. Helium is the second lightest element. It is very common! But scientists did not know it existed until the eclipse allowed them to see it.

In 1915 Albert Einstein wrote his **theory** of relativity. It is his most famous work. He said that light from far away stars bends when it passes by our sun. The sun is too bright for us to see the passing starlight. But it can be photographed during a solar eclipse. During an eclipse in 1919 scientists took photos of the starlight. It bent! Einstein was right.

element—basic substance in chemistry that cannot be split into simpler substances
theory—idea that brings together several hypotheses to explain something

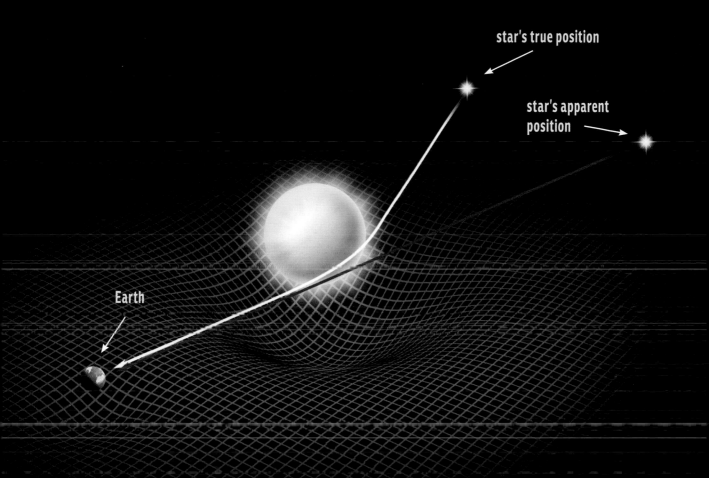

star's true position

star's apparent position

Earth

Coordinated Observations

Scientists continue to study eclipses. They can learn more by working together. Scientists take photos at the same time from many locations. Then they compare the data. They look at how it has changed over time. This helps them learn about changes in the sun and moon.

CHAPTER 4

PREDICTING ECLIPSES

Scientists know the paths that the Earth and moon travel. They also know the speeds of the orbits. Using this data, they predict when and where future eclipses will occur.

Earth sees several eclipses each year. NASA knows all future eclipses until the year 3000. The dates are posted on NASA's website. Anyone can check the calendar. You can find out where to go to watch Earth's next eclipse.

SELECTED ECLIPSE CALENDAR

DATE	TYPE OF ECLIPSE	PLACES WHERE IT WILL BE VISIBLE
Aug 11, 2018	Partial Solar	North/East Europe, North/West Asia, North America, Atlantic Ocean, Arctic
Jan 20 / Jan 21, 2019	Total Lunar	Europe, Asia, Africa, North America, South America, Pacific Ocean, Atlantic Ocean, Indian Ocean, Arctic
Jul 2, 2019	Total Solar	North America, much of South America, Pacific Ocean
Nov 11, 2019	Mercury Transit	South/West Europe, South/West Asia, Africa, much of North America, South America, Indian Ocean, Antarctica
Dec 26, 2019	Annular Solar	East in Europe, much of Asia, North/West Australia, East in Africa, Pacific Ocean, Indian Ocean
May 26, 2021	Total Lunar	South/East Asia, Australia, much of North America, South America, Pacific Ocean, Atlantic Ocean, Indian Ocean, Antarctica
Oct 25, 2022	Partial Solar	Europe, South/West Asia, North/East Africa, Atlantic Ocean

VIEWING AN ECLIPSE

Watching an eclipse is an exciting event. But it cannot be seen from just anywhere. Your part of the planet may not have an eclipse for many years. When one happens in your area, it is a historic event.

Lunar eclipses are easy to watch. You can see them with the naked eye. But you may want to use a telescope. It will let you see the eclipse in more detail. You could also find a local planetarium and see if an eclipse viewing will be hosted there.

Solar eclipses are more difficult. You should never look directly at the sun. Doing so could damage your eyes. It could even cause blindness.

Most people watch a solar eclipse using special glasses or a cardboard viewer. An eclipse viewer has a small hole cut in it. Sunlight shines through the hole and onto a surface. During an eclipse, the moon's shadow moves across this ray of light. With the right tools, you can safely watch your next eclipse.

GLOSSARY

astronomer (uh-STRAH-nuh-muhr)—scientist who studies stars, planets, and other objects in space

corona (kuh-ROH-nuh)—outermost part of the sun's atmosphere

eclipse (i-KLIPS)—when one object in space blocks light and keeps it from shining on another object in space

element (E-luh-muhnt)—basic substance in chemistry that cannot be split into simpler substances

exoplanet (EK-soh-plan-it)—planet that orbits a star outside the solar system

lunar eclipse (LOO-nuhr i-KLIPS)—astronomical event in which Earth's shadow passes over the moon

mythology (mi-THOL-uh-jee)—old or ancient stories told again and again that help connect people with their past

orbit (OR-bit)—path an object follows as it goes around the sun or a planet

orbiter (OR-bit-ur)—spacecraft that orbits a planet or other space objects

solar eclipse (SOH-lur i-KLIPSS)—astronomical event in which the moon passes between the sun and Earth

theory (THEE-ur-ee)—idea that brings together several hypotheses to explain something

READ MORE

Garbe, Suzanne. *The Science Behind Wonders of the Sun: Sun Dogs, Lunar Eclipses, and Green Flash.* The Science Behind Natural Phenomena. North Mankato, Minn.: Capstone Press, 2017.

Hunter, Nick. *Eclipses.* The Night Sky: and Other Amazing Sights. Chicago: Heinemann Library, 2013.

Oxlade, Chris. *The Moon.* Astronaut Travel Guides. Chicago: Raintree, 2013.

INTERNET SITES

Use FactHound to find Internet sites related to this book

Visit *www.facthound.com*

Just type in 9781515787365 and go.

 Check out projects, games and lots more at
www.capstonekids.com

CRITICAL THINKING QUESTIONS

1. What is the difference between a lunar and solar eclipse?

2. Why do scientists study eclipses?

3. If the Earth had no atmosphere, what color would the moon be during a lunar eclipse?

INDEX